MAGNA FAMILY
LIBRARY

LOVERS'
HOROSCOPES

To Sandy and Mollie
– young love

MAGNA FAMILY
LIBRARY

LOVERS' HOROSCOPES

LORI REID

MAGNA BOOKS

First published in the UK
1992 by Ward Lock
a Cassell Imprint
Villiers House, 41/47 Strand, London, WC2N 5JE

This edition has been produced in 1994 for Magna Books,
Magna Road, Wigston, Leicester, LE18 4ZH, UK

For further information about Magna Books please contact:
Magna Books,
Magna Road, Wigston
Leicester LE18 4ZH, UK

ISBN 1-85422-831-5

Typeset by Columns of Reading Ltd

Printed and bound in Finland

CONTENTS

INTRODUCTION

Astrology, derived from the Greek words *astra* and *logos*, together meaning 'the science of the stars', is the study of the planets and their influence on the lives of all living things. This ancient system of knowledge is based on the belief that the patterns made by the planets in the heavens directly correspond to and influence the pattern of the life of an individual.

From earliest times man has studied the heavens, observed the movement of the planets in the firmament and noted how these movements correspond to changes: how the sun affects the seasons, how the moon exerts a gravitational pull on the tides, how the planets in our solar system appear to have a direct effect on the mood and behaviour of humans and animals alike and how, moreover, they seem to have a hand in shaping character and personality according to the time of year in which an individual is born.

To facilitate their study, early astrologers divided the heavens into 12 sections, each one given a name which we collectively know as the signs of the Zodiac. Every planet journeys through the 12 sections in turn. Some, like the Moon, pay a fleeting visit of two to three days in each sign, whilst others, such as Saturn, may stay there for two to three years.

The sun takes a whole year to travel through all the signs, from Aries to Pisces, and whether a person is a Leo, a Scorpio, a Capricorn or whatever, depends on where the sun was at the moment of their birth. Moreover, by carefully studying the positions of the planets at the moment of an individual's birth, an astrologer is able to compile a personal natal horoscope which can be interpreted to give detailed information about that person and guidance in every aspect of their life.

It used to be that all learned men studied astrology, and its concepts were part of everyday life, even for the ordinary man in the street, who recognised a relationship between the stars and their cosmic influence on life. Medicine, for example, was strongly tied up with astrology, and a physician would consult the patient's natal chart before embarking on a course of treatment. Even herbs for healing were picked and administered strictly according to planetary lore.

In fact, astrology was such a respected and established branch of learning during the Middle Ages that not only was it taught at university but most royal houses in Europe, too, had a court astrologer, who would advise on daily matters as well as on global events.

Mainly because of religious intolerance, however, astrology in the West later underwent a decline. In the East, where the art is more sympathetic to Oriental philosophy, its popularity has never been in question. Today in India and China astrologers play a major role in all aspects of personal, domestic and commercial life. Parents have the natal charts of their newborn infants erected at birth; business transactions, new enterprises, journeys, meetings and the like are often embarked upon only after close astrological scrutiny has established the propitious moment.

A couple, before even contemplating marriage, will have their respective horoscopes analysed to check for compatibility, point out their weak spots, the positive and negative character traits that will reflect on their relationship, the general events and trends that are likely to occur. The astrologer here will even pinpoint a suitable date on which the wedding should take place.

Happily, although astrology is still a controversial subject, the last 150 years or so have seen a growing resurgence of interest in it throughout the West. Modern studies carried out by eminent scientists are not only beginning to validate some of the claims of astrological teaching, but also giving it the respectability it deserves. Nowadays, astrologers are consulted in all areas of decision-making, from psychological counselling to advising on the stock exchange. Even Nancy Reagan was found to consult her personal astrologer when she was First Lady of America — the closest thing in modern times, some might say, to those royal court astrologers of the Middle Ages!

Whether we believe in it or not, it is an indisputable fact that astrology has been practised worldwide for many thousands of years, and on that basis alone it cannot be simply dismissed out of hand. Certainly, from time immemorial, lovers in particular have consulted the stars about their fate, to find out when they would meet and marry the man or woman of their dreams. Or they might attempt to gauge the suitability of their mate, reach a deeper understanding of their partner or determine whether their love for each other would stand the test of time.

Indeed, emotional problems and questions about relationships probably account for a good sixty to seventy per cent of all queries that a consultant astrologer is presented with. And astrology can provide many of the answers as it is able to establish links between two people's characters and personalities, throw up similarities and discrepancies, highlight their innermost dreams and aspirations and show trends and directions which their lives together would take.

Although this kind of in-depth analysis is obtained through the information revealed by an individual's personal birthchart, there are still many general infer-ences that we can each make about ourselves and our lovers simply by knowing the date of birth and consequently the sun sign under which a person is born. Even this sparse information can reveal an enormous amount, not only about general character, personality and disposition, but also about mental and physical compatibility between the signs, tastes, preferences, likes and dislikes – many of the things, in fact, that will give a pretty good idea as to whether two people are likely to hit it off together or not.

ON THE CUSP

When people say they are 'on the cusp' it means they were born either during the first few days or within the last few days of a sun sign. For example, someone born on 19 March would be on the cusp of Pisces and Aries. As a result, they are a mixture of the characteristics of both signs. So, whereas Pisceans might normally be shy, withdrawn, reticent and unsure of themselves, being born here adds the Arien influence of energy, courage and greater confidence to their nature.

If you or your lover were born on the cusp, read both signs either side of your date of birth as you will find that elements from each will apply equally to you.

LOVE AMONGST THE STARS

ARIES

21 March – 20 April

Symbol: The Ram
Ruler: Mars
Element: Fire

KEYNOTES TO CHARACTER

Active, dramatic, courageous, pioneering, like to be leaders, quick to learn, plenty of initiative, masses of enthusiasm, aggressive and impatient, tactless, insensitive, hot-headed.

THE ARIAN LOVER

Arians are impulsive people and often fall in love at first sight. They are enthusiastic, generous and affectionate lovers, rather romantic and sentimental but sometimes fool-hardy in their pursuit of love. The man who pitches himself out of an aeróplane, skis down a mountain slope, scales the side of a building and jumps in through the window of the apartment at the top, simply to leave a box of chocolates for his lady-love has to be an Arian!

Dynamic leaders, these fiery extroverts are ardent lovers with masses of sexual energy and drive. In their relationships they need to play a dominant role. With their strength of character, they need an equally strong partner. Anyone too weak or too passive would simply irritate Arian subjects who, unless well-matched in this way, soon become bored and restless and look for adventure and stimulation elsewhere.

Their relationships have to be exciting, challenging, alive, full of activity. And if partners are sporty, all the better, for then energetic pursuits can be taken-up together. If not, the partners must recognise the Arian's need for adventure, and cheerfully pack their sports kits for them, even now and again going along to watch, heart in mouth, as the fearless and courageous Arian struggles for conquest and supremacy.

Ladies of the sign will be just as dominant and eager as their male counterparts. In love-making, they are direct and to the point, often taking the initiative. They are go-getters, true powers-behind-the-throne, pushing their men towards success. Above all, an Arian lady will consider herself equal to any man, and though passionate and loving, will maintain a certain independence. In fact, the Arian character typifies the spirit of feminism.

If you are interested in capturing the heart of an Arian you have to play hard to get. Keep them guessing and keep them chasing; that way you will be sure to keep them interested. Lie down submissively at their feet, though, and any self-respecting Arian will simply step over you and keep right on going. The thrill of the chase, the anticipation, the object of desire just that little bit out of reach, is how an Arian likes to play the game of love.

CHARACTER FAULTS

Arians can be immensely impatient. There's always a feeling of straining at the leash with this child of the Zodiac. Quick-tempered and impulsive, they act first and ask questions later – much later, in fact. And when they do they aren't exactly the most tactful of people!

But perhaps the biggest fault they possess is due to their placement amongst the twelve signs. Aries is the first sign, it is the awakener, coming at a time when new life is stirring, when all things are burgeoning and thrusting. This characteristic of being first is thus reflected in the sons and daughters of Aries and manifests itself in a tendency to egocentricity and selfishness.

HOW TO SPOT YOUR ARIAN LOVER

The popular name for Aries is the 'Ram' and, true to their symbol, those born in this sign invariably possess thick, fleecy hair around long faces with very wide foreheads. They like comfortable clothes that won't impede their movements, so often go for the sporty or casual look in dress. Arians, more than any one else, have a penchant for hats.

Red is their favourite colour, and many ladies of this sign will use this to accessorize their outfits. Red also features in their favourite jewellery, with rubies and bloodstones being suitable precious stones for them. Their perfume must be bold, fresh and dramatic to reflect their personalities.

OTHER LOVERS WHO SHARE THE SIGN

Kingsley Amis
Alan Ayckbourn
Jeffrey Archer
Jane Asher
Severiano Ballesteros
Dirk Bogarde
Doris Day
Paul Daniels
Peter Davison
Clare Francis
David Frost
James Garner
Sir John Gielgud
Hannah Gordon
Alec Guiness
Gloria Hunniford
David Icke
Elton John

Gorden Kaye
Penelope Keith
Neil Kinnock
Martyn Lewis
Nicholas Lyndhurst
Donald MacCormick
Spike Milligan
Hayley Mills
Dudley Moore
Michael Parkinson
Eric Porter
Peter Powell
Andre Previn
Omar Sharif
Valerie Singleton
Peter Snow
David Steel
Peter Ustinov

TAURUS

21 April – 21 May

Symbol: The Bull
Ruler: Venus
Element: Earth

KEYNOTES TO CHARACTER

Hard-working, charming, common-sense, practical, patient, affectionate, loves material comforts, plodding, reliable, artistic, stubborn, self-indulgent, possessive, resentful, greedy, materialistic.

THE TAUREAN LOVER

Taureans may not be considered the greatest lovers in the Zodiac but they are surely some of the most romantic. In love, they can be passionate and sensual.

Indeed, sensuality is one of Taurus' salient characteristics. And it is this very sensuality that makes them enjoy love-making so much – kissing, caressing, erotically extending the fore-play because they derive such pleasure from the sheer physical contact.

When it comes to serious relationships, though, they tend not to look so much for passion as security. In fact, for them, security is the top priority. The ability to provide financial, material and emotional stability is what they will be looking for in a relationship. Offer a lady Taurean love wrapped in luxury, and you have a faithful partner for the rest of your life!

But, coupled with the need for security, Taureans also expect faithfulness and loyalty from their partners. Indeed, members of this sign can make the most loyal and tolerant partners, to the point where they would continue to persevere in a marriage long after the relationship has irretrievably broken down.

Don't ever try to hood-wink your Taurean lover, for they are shrewd and will see right through you. And if you tell lies, even the tiniest white lie, they're sure to make you regret it! You see, honesty in a relationship is of paramount importance to those born with their sun in this sign.

In general, Taureans tend to be warm-hearted and fairly easy-going. Pleasant and affable, they have a natural charm that attracts the opposite sex.

Taureans are physically attractive – the men are usually distinctively handsome and the women rather soft, sensual and sexy. Indeed, beauty is important to both males and females, so they usually team up with a good-looking partner and spare no expense to make their surroundings both comfortable and beautiful. Much of their money, in fact will be invested in lovely artefacts for the home.

If you've fallen in love with a Taurean you can be sure of a strong, solid and secure companion. He will provide for you, be faithful, take delight in showering you with gifts, cosset you and pamper to your every need. Your Taurean sweetheart will be responsive to your needs, provide a warm, loving and comfortable home, delight you with her sensuality and doggedly follow you to the ends of the earth. And if you want to especially surprise your lover, think of food – their greatest weakness. A splendid banquet is the surest way to his heart. A box of hand-made chocolates, wrapped in gold paper tied with a huge satin bow, will have her eating out of your hand, well ... for the rest of the evening, at least!

CHARACTER FAULTS

The biggest fault of your Taurean lover, as if you hadn't already noticed, is stubbornness. Once these people get a notion into their heads, it becomes nigh-on impossible to shift it. You can argue until you're blue in the face with them but they simply dig in their heels and just refuse to budge.

Possessiveness is another negative characteristic. Once they have wooed and conquered, they want to possess their partners, body and soul. If their partners so much as stray for just one moment, smile a little too intimately at another woman, perhaps, or appear to flirt with another man at a party, the Taurean will feel utterly betrayed. And boy, can they kick up a stink about it when you get home!

Though they are in general hard workers, their very sensuality can make them sloppy and lazy. They can become self-indulgent, spoiling themselves silly, giving-in to their enormous appetites, which, in some Taureans, can simply turn into downright greed.

HOW TO SPOT YOUR TAUREAN LOVER

Think of the bull and then apply its characteristics. Taureans are often stocky, with a predominant neck – either a thick, bull-neck or, sometimes quite conversely, a long swan-like neck. Taurean ladies will often draw attention to their necks by tying ribbons or bows around them or wearing lacy collars. Their hair is often thick and curly.

They tend to favour the classical look and sometimes may appear a little old-fashioned. Frills and furbelows, pastel colours and soft blues are especially popular with them. The stones of the sign are sapphire and emerald. Perfumes to suit would be florally with a delicate and feminine fragrance.

OTHER LOVERS WHO SHARE THE SIGN

Francesca Annis
David Attenborough
Anne Baxter
Alan Bennett
Eric Bristow
Joe Brown
Cher
George Cole
Henry Cooper
Michael Fish
Ella Fitzgerald
Susan Hampshire

HM The Queen
Glenda Jackson
Maureen Lipman
Joanna Lumley
Jeremy Paxman
Pope John Paul II
David Shepherd
Selina Scott
Miriam Stoppard
Barbra Streisand
Toyah Willcox
Stevie Wonder
Victoria Wood

GEMINI

22 May – 21 June

Symbol:	The Twins
Ruler:	Mercury
Element:	Air

KEYNOTES TO CHARACTER

Need for variety and stimulation, vivacious, versatile, adaptable, quick-witted, clever, studious, deceitful, unreliable, touch of nervous instability, superficial, excellent at bluffing.

THE GEMINIAN LOVER

Of all the signs of the Zodiac, Gemini is the least reliable when it comes to love and marriage. The problem is that they have an extremely low boredom-threshold. In life, they need novelty and variety, and in relationships they need a partner who will be stimulating, entertaining and challenging.

Geminians make lively and amusing partners and are great fun to have around. Peter Pan types, versatile and adaptable, they have the knack of getting-on with just about everyone. But the most important thing for them is communication. They are great talkers – many are born with a natural 'gift of the gab' – many make excellent writers, and many find their way into the media, in one form or another. As long as they have someone with whom to communicate, they are in their element.

So, in partnerships they will be looking for someone on their wavelength, someone who is lively, witty and intelligent. Indeed intelligence is more likely to attract a Geminian than a sexy bimbo would any day. Sex is really not that important to them – if they can achieve mind-touch with another person, body-touch doesn't even get a look-in. A Gemini is happier sitting up all night discussing politics, religion, literature, or whatever is the current interest, than romping the night away between the sheets!

Hence Geminians' attitude to sex is rather casual. For them, sex is something trivial, something that can be taken or left, something that doesn't require a great deal of emotional investment. They are likely to have a good many sexual adventures for they are fickle and flirtatious, even when married. To them extra-marital sex simply does not add up to a sin, it's simply a way of communicating with someone, just as you might have a chat with a neighbour across the garden wall.

Partners, lovers and spouses of Geminians have to develop a good deal of tolerance with these gregarious, silver-tongued individuals. They also have to learn some ingenious tricks if they want to stay one step ahead and hold on to their fickle and slippery partners. If they can keep-up the intellectual buzz, share the variety of interests, maintain an alluring mystique, and turn an occasional blind eye to their partners' peccadillos and indiscretions, there is every hope of a lasting relationship, and one that will be filled with entertainment, sparkle and fun.

If their partners cannot be so tolerant, or indeed so amusing and stimulating, the Geminian is likely to look elsewhere. It does seem to be a very tall order, as can be seen in their rather poor record of stable marriages.

CHARACTER FAULTS

The problem with Geminians is their dual nature. This sign is symbolised by 'The Twins' hence the attributes of duplicity and changeability. Geminians have been described through the ages as elusive, two-faced, crafty and cunning. They are good at spinning a yarn and, with Mercurial cleverness, have a tendency to bend the rules to suit themselves. In the modern idiom, they are not averse to being 'economical with the truth'. And they are darn clever at covering their traces!

When it comes to relationships, their low boredom-threshold, their restlessness and need for change and variety can jeopardise their partnerships and their marriages, especially as they are such uncontrollable flirts.

HOW TO SPOT YOUR GEMINIAN LOVER

Geminians are easily recognised by their quick, nervous, fidgety, bird-like movements and mannerisms. They are especially noted for their bright, alert eyes that don't miss a thing, and their ears may be prominant. Their buzzing need for news, views and communication means they love anything that's new and the latest fashion. Ladies of the sign, often possess masses of clothes, which they mix and match to suit their versatile temperament. They also enjoy having their hair done in the style of the minute.

Yellows, white and gold are the Geminian colours, and the birthstones are agate, jade and diamonds. Like their catholic taste for clothes, perfumes of all sorts are liked by Ms Gemini with the emphasis on quantity rather than quality so they can choose whichever to wear according to their mood of the day.

OTHER LOVERS WHO SHARE THE SIGN

Richard Baker
James Bolam
Katie Boyle
Tony Britton
Simon Callow
Bob Champion
Joan Collins
Wendy Craig
Gemma Craven
Paul Eddington
Denholm Elliott

Duncan Goodhew
HRH The Duke of Edinburgh
Peter Jones
Christopher Lee
Paul McCartney
Bob Monkhouse
Robert Powell
Beryl Reid
Suzi Quatro
Richard Todd

CANCER

22 June – 22 July

Symbol: The Crab
Ruler: The Moon
Element: Water

KEYNOTES TO CHARACTER

Domestic, home-loving, need security and stability, sensitive, kind, compassionate, cautious, caring, moody, clinging, unforgiving.

THE CANCERIAN LOVER

Of all the Zodiac's children, Cancerians are the most home-loving. They only function happily when they have a warm, secure and loving relationship to fall back on. They are extremely emotional and sensitive individuals, who form very deep bonds with those they love. Family ties are important to them too, many having an especially close rapport with their mothers. Cancerians can live very happily in an extended family network, marrying but settling back into the family home, with brothers, sisters and other relatives all living close-by.

Ruled as they are by the moon, Cancerians are domestically happy types, loving and caring, protective but also possessive. Many love their homes so much that they choose a job which they can do from home, or set up an office in their spare room, or open a business in a shed in the back garden. Many are in their element in the kitchen, becoming fine cooks and excellent chefs.

Romantically, a Cancerian partner will make a warm and cuddly friend. They adore romance and are tender and gentle lovers. They can appear shy initially when meeting people of the opposite sex, but once they fall in love they give everything they've got to that relationship because when a Cancerian falls in love, it's forever. It has been said that Cancerians and marriage were made for each other, and indeed a lonely and unloved Cancerian is one. hell of a miserable person.

When looking for a mate, Cancerians will be drawn to gentle and kind people who will provide security. Being shy, they are likely to be attracted to warm, extrovert types, who complement their own personalities. Great intellect is not necessarily a characteristic they require in a lover, but they will look for a partner who will provide plenty of love and will appreciate their sensitivity and vulnerability. And, once these gentle children of the moon find the right man or woman, they make faithful, life-long and devoted partners.

In marriage, male Cancerians will look for a partner who will mother them.

Ladies of the sign are only too happy to mother not only their children but also their men-folk. They have a certain fragility and a strong femininity that men find irresistible and that brings out the protective instinct in the male. As both sexes mature into the relationship, they become practical in the home and thrifty with money. That's not to say they are necessarily mean, but they are careful with the household accounts.

If you are planning to wed your beloved Cancerian, remember that they are very conventional at heart. This means that in marriage they expect to follow traditional, stereotype sex roles – he Tarzan, she Jane. So, if you have more avante-garde ideas about the meaning of relationships, perhaps you have strong feminist tendencies, or are drawn by the image of the 'New Man', then beware for there are certain to be serious clashes of opinion here!

CHARACTER FAULTS

Being ruled by the moon, with its fluctuations, its periods of waxing and waning, the Cancerian will inevitably reflect the planet's changes. And indeed, the most annoying part of the Cancerian character is their changeable moods – up one minute and down the next.

For many people, a good memory is an asset but for Cancerians, their long and detailed memories may be considered a definite minus point. This is because they have an infinite capacity for remembering every single slight that was ever levelled at them. In fact, they are quite capable of keeping a mental tally of the minutest wrongs they have had to suffer. They could tick off in their minds who crossed them, when it happened and how. And they are likely to carry those slights around with them for a very long time.

Furthermore, they are not likely to forgive easily either. In fact, it probably wouldn't be too far from the truth to say that the first person ever to start a feud must have been a Cancerian!

HOW TO SPOT YOUR CANCERIAN LOVER

The facial characteristics of these people are heavily influenced by the moon. Many of them have round faces, pale skin and a milky-white complexion. In general, their facial features are small and neat. Cancerian ladies often adore romantic, antique clothing. Of today's fashions, they prefer simple, uncomplicated styles. For evening wear, they seem to like low-cut outfits which give a tantalizing glimpse of their cleavage!

Silver, white, ice-blue and rose – subtle colours to enhance their femininity. Jewellery is special to Cancerian ladies and, as with their love of clothes from a bygone age, they take great pleasure in collecting antique jewellery. Pearls and moonstones are especially suitable for this sign ruled by the moon. Perfume should be light and fragrant, wholesome and even old-fashioned, such as lavender. Anything heavy or spicy would simply overpower the image of this delicate lady.

OTHER LOVERS WHO SHARE THE SIGN

Tim Brooke-Taylor
Mel Brooks
Alastair Burnet
Barbara Cartland
Bill Cosby
Kid Jensen
HRH Prince Michael of Kent
HRH The Princess of Wales
HRH Prince William
Bonnie Langford
Sue Lawley
Gina Lollobrigida
Bill Oddie
David Owen
Maggie Philbin
Esther Rantzen
Prunella Scales
Meryl Streep
Mollie Sugden
Donald Sutherland
Virginia Wade
Colin Wilson

LEO

23 July – 23 August

Symbol: The Lion
Ruler: The Sun
Element: Fire

KEYNOTES TO CHARACTER

Aristocratic air, generous, warm and loving, confident, proud, arrogant, condescending, selfish, dominant, conceited.

THE LEO LOVER

Leos are dynamic individuals and fiery lovers. Passion is a by-word of this sign. Big-hearted, generous and affectionate, Leo men are courteous and chivalrous towards women in general, and to their partners in particular. Kings of the jungle and, for that matter, of the

Zodiac too, they have a regal air, possessing what might be described as courtly manners in the wooing and winning of their lady-loves.

There's something rather grand about Leo ladies. Ruled by the Sun, they like to shine and radiate their warmth to all around. These female felines like more than a touch of the *dolce vita* in their lives. They do nothing by halves. Extravagant, they pull out all the stops, lavishing their generosity and bonhomie on all who come within their sphere.

Like their symbol the Lion, Leos are proud, courageous people and carry about them, whatever their circumstances, a sense of dignity which marks them out from their fellow men.

At work, their organisational skills soon become apparent and they quickly show that they're born leaders with a charistmatic ability to command respect. They are eminently suited to responsibility so they naturally rise to the top, very often landing themselves in positions of prestige and authority.

Both sexes of this sign have a tendency to gravitate to centre-stage; they are simply at their best in the glare of the spotlight receiving the adultation and applause they feel is theirs by right. Indeed, an over-shadowed Leo is rather a sad sight!

Natives of this sunny sign are very sexually attractive people. Warm and loving, it is unusual to find a Leo without a partner for they are instinctively drawn towards a mate, to someone to share their love, to love and be loved in return.

In marriage, they make exuberant, loyal and faithful partners. Impulsively full of fun and excitement, playful like little lion cubs, open, sunny, attractive and optimistic – there is never a dull moment with a Leo around. Providing, that is, they can lord it over their homes and their families and be made to feel the centre of attention.

In fact, just as in the jungle, so the lion in his home needs to feel he is 'king of the castle'. When happily married and settled, he will radiate warmth, generosity and his protective light upon all who depend on him. Indeed, a happily married Leo may justly be described as not so much a lion, more a pussy-cat at heart, purring contentedly as they bask in the central security of their lair.

CHARACTER FAULTS

The major Leonine fault stems from their self-pride which can, at times, turn to conceit. The feeling of self-importance brings out the bossy, domineering and arrogant side of the Leo nature. At their worst Leos may be caught looking down their noses from their regal heights patronising those less fortunate than themselves.

Another negative trait is the Leonine vanity or ego – which is vast and which demands constant reassurance. Without this vital confirmation, Leos can visibly wither, their egos deflate and their self-pride disintegrate into tatters. This urgent need for reassurance renders the Leo susceptible to flattery and open to any amount of insincere fawning.

HOW TO SPOT YOUR LEO LOVER

Leos can be spotted a mile away by their regal bearing. They hold themselves with confidence and walk with their heads held up high. They have a veritable mane of luxuriant, flowing hair. But the biggest give-away is their faces which, reminiscent of the feline king of the jungle, have high cheekbones and a certain cat-like *'je ne sais quoi'*.

Leos love rich clothes and often have a dramatic sense of style. They are lavish in their application of glitter and bright fiery colours that compel attention. In fact, all the warm colours of fire are preferred – gold, orange, bronze. Ruby, amber and tourmaline are their stones, and rich, spicy fragranges their choice of perfume.

OTHER LOVERS WHO SHARE THE SIGN

Neil Armstrong
Honor Blackman
Fidel Castro
Steve Davis
David Essex
Georgina Hale
Joan Hickson
HRH Princess Margaret
HRH The Princess Royal
HM Queen Elizabeth, the Queen Mother
P.D. James

Martin Jarvis
Diane Keen
Danny La Rue
Ian McCaskill
Trevor McDonald
Nick Ross
Willie Rushton
Clive Sinclair
Lizzie Webb
Alan Whicker
Terry Wogan

VIRGO

24 August – 22 September

Symbol: The Virgin
Ruler: Mercury
Element: Earth

KEYNOTES TO CHARACTER

Clean, neat, tidy, fussy, orderly, house-proud, loyal worker, perfectionist, hypercritical, self-righteous, prissy, tendency to complain.

THE VIRGOAN LOVER

Virgoans have extremely high standards of excellence. Indeed, they may be considered the perfectionists of the Zodiac. Down-to-earth and practical, they are not easily swept off their feet and, although loving types, they do find it hard to be demonstrative and fight shy of exposing their feelings.

In matters of love, they have been referred to as the 'virgins of the Zodiac'. Some might even describe them as prudish. Unlike the more fiery signs, these could not, in a thousand years, be considered smouldering, erotic types. In fact, sexually, they need to be gently kindled, slowly and carefully brought to boiling point. Yet still they will not lose their heads, never stray from that cool reason and critical judgement that Virgoans are so reputed to possess. It would not be too far-fetched to say that to turn-on a Virgoan sexually can be a bit of an up-hill struggle.

Building up a relationship with a Virgoan can be a slow business. Romantic attachments for them often develop out of a friendship, through professional contact or business acquaintanceship. Ruled by Mercury, they enjoy discussion and debate, so perhaps long chats far into the night might be one way to spark-off their interest.

If you really want to impress your Virgoan, make sure that you are turned out neatly, that your flat or house is meticulously clean and tidy and that you cross all the necessary 't's' and dot all the appropriate 'i's', for these people are perfectionists and hypercritical when it comes to detail, cleanliness and hygiene. A fiercely strong sense of order makes them compulsively tidy, not only in their environment but in their person as well. They can be very house-proud, and in their manners and dress, always correct, modest, tactful and circumspect.

The chances are that you will meet your Virgoan lover in a hospital, or working for one of the branches of the welfare service, for they seem to naturally gravitate towards work which entails looking after others. They make wonderful carers, being kind and ever helpful to those in need. If you need a helping hand or a good turn, the Virgoan is your man, or woman.

In marriage Virgoans make solid and reliable partners, quietly loving and caring for their homes and families. They are hard workers, never sitting still for a minute, and always finding jobs to do no matter how tired they may feel. 'The devil makes work for idle hands' seems very much a motto befitting these people born with their sun in this sign.

CHARACTER FAULTS

The most negative aspect of the Virgoan is their critical nature. Because they are perfectionists and idealistic in themselves, they find it hard to accept that other people may not quite come up to their standards of excellence.

Pernickety and fastidious in the extreme, they can become nit-picking and carping as they grow older, nagging their less-conscientious spouses to distraction.

HOW TO SPOT YOUR VIRGO LOVER

True Virgoans are characterised by their clean, neat and tidy appearance, and loathe being dirty or looking unkempt. It is amazing how they can go through a whole day and still emerge looking fresh and uncrumpled! The child who comes out of school spotless and immaculate simply has to be a Virgo.

Ladies of the sign are very modest in their dress, preferring to blend into the background rather than project themselves forward, so they will never be seen in anything outlandish, frivolous or ostentatious. Both Mr and Ms Virgo like simple, comfortable and easy-to-wear clothes, and if they resemble the seasons in their colour, print or design, so much the better.

All shades of brown with their associations with Nature and Mother Earth, suit Virgoans. Their birthstones are sardonyx, diamond and Jasper. Perfumes should be light and florally.

OTHER LOVERS WHO SHARE THE SIGN

Russ Abbot
Pamela Armstrong
Sean Connery
Dana
Linda Gray
HRH Prince Harry
Lenny Henry

Jeremy Irons
Sophia Loren
Desmond Lynam
Cliff Robertson
Sir Harry Secombe
Twiggy
Raquel Welch

LIBRA

23 September – 23 October

Symbol: The Scales
Ruler: Venus
Element: Air

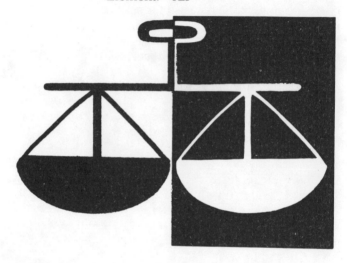

KEYNOTES TO CHARACTER

Need for balance and symmetry, elegant, fair, artistic, indecisive, lazy, extravagant, sycophantic, smarmy.

THE LIBRAN LOVER

Librans are very romantic people. The practice of serenading a beautiful lady with verse and song surely must have been invented by a man born under this sign.

Indeed, Librans of both sexes can get quite swept away by their own sentimentality, often falling in love with love itself rather than truly falling head over heels for another person.

It is because of this romanticism that they can so very easily become infatuated, often marrying for all the wrong reasons, only to regret it later in life.

Librans are often described as charming. Most are good-looking, with an easy, pleasant manner that attracts others to them. In general, they love all things good and beautiful in life: good food, good wine, good companionship, beautiful music, beautiful clothes, beautiful surroundings. To find themselves surrounded by ugliness, or forced to work in unpleasant circumstances or amongst uncongenial people, will make Librans physically ill. Indeed, unpleasantness of any sort will completely unsettle them and make their lives a misery.

Just as the symbol for Libra is the scales, so Librans need harmony and balance in their lives. Peace at any price is their motto, for they cannot abide discord in any form. The scales not only symbolise balance but justice, too, for another Libran preoccupation is the pursuit of fair play, weighing-up good and bad, right and wrong.

In love, they are thoughtful and caring, concerned about making everything nice for their other half. Gentle lovers, they are sympathetic and understanding partners, tactful, charming in the extreme and always seeking harmony in their relationships. So much so, in fact, that they will positively shun any emotional discord, actively retreating from, rather than confronting, the source of conflict.

Generally, though independent types, Librans do well in a happy and settled relationship, for they need the emotional stability and security that a special partner in life can bring.

CHARACTER FAULTS

The biggest fault of Librans is their downright laziness. Of all the signs of the Zodiac, members of this one are the least likely to roll up their sleeves and pitch in when it comes to tackling dirty or unpleasant jobs. They simply don't like to get their hands dirty and are brilliant at devising avoidance strategies, slipping away with such charm that you hardly realise you've been left holding the baby!

Their second biggest fault is their sense of self-pity. Many Librans do suffer from a sense of personal injustice, believing that they are mis-judged, or that life is simply unfair to them, and as a result they may winge and whine and become quite resentful.

Other negative characteristics include indecisiveness and, in some cases, insincerity. The latter may be a consequence of the Libran charm, which at times can flip into downright smarminess. But when it comes to emotional matters, it may be the Libran tendency to be critical of others which can all too often be so detrimental to their relationships.

HOW TO SPOT YOUR LIBRAN LOVER

Librans are often tall and slender. Invariably elegant, they can be spotted by their good taste in clothes, which are often expensive, well-cut and soft to the touch. Librans go in for romantic fashions, so you are unlikely to see a Libran in too heavily-tailored or very strictly-cut clothes. Rather, they will wear clothes that are flowing and somewhat reminiscent of the Pre-Raphaelite look. The one big Libran give-away is their straight hair, which some might describe as lank.

Pastel shades, light blues and pinks are often chosen by Librans for their outfits. Sapphire and opals are their birthstones. Ladies of the sign enjoy a sophisticated perfume and one which is usually very expensive.

OTHER LOVERS WHO SHARE THE SIGN

Ronnie Barker
Peter Bowles
Melvyn Bragg
Max Bygraves
Barbara Castle
Sebastian Coe
Sandy Gall
Graham Greene
Robert Hardy
James Herriot
Patricia Hodge
Sir Michael Hordern
HRH The Duke of Kent
HRH The Duchess of York

Deborah Kerr
Evel Knivel
Felicity Kendal
Magnus Magnusson
Marcello Mastroianni
Linda McCartney
Roger Moore
George Peppard
Christopher Reeve
Anneka Rice
Cliff Richard
Donald Sinden
Margaret Thatcher
Bill Tidy

SCORPIO

24 October – 22 November

Symbol: The Scorpion
Ruler: Pluto
Element: Water

KEYNOTES TO CHARACTER

Sexy, passionate, strong personality, discerning, intense, magnetic, deep, jealous, envious, secretive, sting-in-the-tail.

THE SCORPIO LOVER

Often described as the sexiest sign of the Zodiac, people born with their sun in Scorpio have strong, powerful personalities. Deep and passionate, they are rather like volcanoes – seemingly still and controlled on the surface but, underneath, a boiling inferno of emotion.

Because of this depth to their personalities, a delicious aura of mystery surrounds them. Lady Scorpios are enigmatic, sultry *femmes fatales*. The men are magnetic and charismatic. Both have a penetrating gaze with which they fix and mesmerize their adversaries.

Intensity is a word most often associated with Scorpios, for these are serious people who feel deeply, love passionately and work single-mindedly. In fact, they throw themselves heart-and-soul into whatever activity they undertake.

Intellectually, they are analytical types, making excellent psychologists for they possess a deep understanding of the workings of the mind. Psychoanalysis, investigative, forensic or detective work, anything that requires logical consideration, digging and delving out facts, working out problems, all will fascinate them and keep their complex, multi-faceted minds busy for hours on end. Once they get the bit between their teeth, you can be sure that they simply won't let go until they feel they have reached a satisfactory conclusion.

They love with the same intensity and single-mindedness as they tackle everything else. It is for this reason that Scorpios are reputed to be passionate lovers. Sex is very important to the members of this sign who are born, it would seem, with an ardent libido. Passion and sensuality are dramatic qualities that go hand-in-hand with the Scorpio temperament and way of life.

When they find a suitable mate, they make caring and protective partners. Gentle and loving, they are fiercely loyal and endlessly solicitous to those they love.

When it comes to relationships, however, Scorpios take an all-or-nothing attitude to love. When they fall in love, they give everything they've got – one hundred percent. But, if crossed, whether in matters of the heart or even in everyday affairs, Scorpios can be ruthless and vindictive.

If you do happen to cross a Scorpio, beware! For this is when that scorpionic sting in the tail will lash out with deadly aim and precision. If for one moment you think you have antagonised a Scorpio and got away with it – think again, for this is not the sort of person who will forgive or, for that matter, forget. It may take years, but they will quietly bide their time, all the while rumbling and smouldering with their fury deep inside, for they don't mind waiting, however long it takes, to settle a score and get even with you. And when the moment is right, when you are off your guard and least expect it then, quite cold-bloodedly, they will strike their lethal blow of revenge.

CHARACTER FAULTS

Much of the negative side of the Scorpionic temperament is bound up with that intensity of feeling. Their worst character traits are their jealousy and possessiveness. Just as they love passionately, so they can hate with equal ferocity and, as described above, if crossed, that sting can be lethal – don't ever underestimate their wrath – for they would go to any lengths to get even. 'Revenge is mine', said the Lord, but Scorpios believe if there is a divine right to revenge it has to belong to them!

Jealousy is really the biggest problem as it can also arouse another bad side of the Scorpionic character – an explosive and often devastating temper. Thank heaven that, in general, Scorpios are masters and mistresses of self-control.

HOW TO SPOT YOUR SCORPIO LOVER

If you ever meet someone whose penetrating gaze seems to bore right through you, then you're probably face to face with a Scorpio. Other than that, they invariably have masses of thick hair and are noticeably intense in their manner. They dress to kill in a sultry and sensual way and with an overall air of mystery and excitement.

Dark red is their colour, and their birthstones are rubies and cornelians. When it comes to perfume the warmer, the spicier, the more exotic it is, the better!

OTHER LOVERS WHO SHARE THE SIGN

Jeremy Brett
John Cleese
Alistair Cooke
Tom Conti
Sharron Davies
Sir Robin Day
David Dimbleby
Nigel Dempster
Ken Dodd
Linda Evans
Fenella Fielding
Bill Giles

Peter Hall
Goldie Hawn
HRH The Prince of Wales
Ludovic Kennedy
Walter Kronkite
Cleo Lane
Lulu
Francois Mitterrand
Sue Pollard
Jimmy Saville
Peter Seabrook
June Whitfield

SAGITTARIUS

23 November – 21 December

Symbol: The Archer
Ruler: Jupiter
Element: Fire

KEYNOTES TO CHARACTER

Enthusiastic, optimistic, open, independent, free-and-easy, idealistic, sincere, positive, sometimes prophetic, untidy, impulsive, live in a whirl-wind, brusque.

THE SAGITTARIAN LOVER

Sagittarians are the most independent and freedom-loving members of the Zodiac. Unconventional, relaxed, friendly and easy-going, they breeze through life in a rather casual manner, often making up their own rules and regulations are they go along.

The freedom to think for themselves and to come and go as they please are important to members of this sign. Like their opposites, the Geminians, they are restless individuals. Often impulsive, Sagittarians need adventure and excitement for they cannot abide the humdrum monotony of routine which, they feel, dulls the senses and stultifies the brain.

Activity is one of the keywords associated with Sagittarians. Indeed, many are sporty individuals and even those who don't actively pursue a regular sport, still enjoy being in the great outdoors, walking, rambling, hiking and riding. In fact, both exercise and plenty of fresh air are essential for a happy and healthy Archer.

Mentally, these people are active too. They have perspicacious minds, strongly intuitive and capable of profound, philosophical thought. Some are born wise, some develop wisdom through their lives. Most show a deep understanding of the human condition and of how people work. In most things they are tolerant and broadminded, taking a liberal, live-and-let-live attitude in life.

Bon viveurs, they have a great gusto for life and live it to the full – their large appetites are often to the detriment of their liver, not to mention their hips and thighs, which have a tendency to broaden with age due to a growing penchant for rich food and good wine!

As friends they are versatile, full of bonhomie and generous to a fault. They are also amusing companions as they have a wonderful sense of humour, even to the point of laughing at themselves and their own foibles. They are well-known for their honesty, their openness and a frankness which can, sometimes, upset those around them who are more tender and sensitive and so perhaps can't take the raw truth as stolidly on the chin as their thicker-skinned companions.

With their freedom-loving ideals and their somewhat light-hearted attitude to life, many Sagittarians are prone to the 'Casanova' instinct and enjoy several casual affairs in their time. As lovers, they can be exciting and great fun for they are adventurous and prone to impulsiveness. For instance, they adore travel and so may decide, at a moment's notice, to whisk their partners off for a romantic weekend in Paris. Or it might be that they find romance, or the very man or woman of their dreams, on one of their many trips overseas.

When it comes to serious relationships, the biggest hurdle of all for Sagittarians is coming to terms with their need for independence; the very thought of being pinned down or over-burdened with responsibility is absolute anathema to them. Indeed, it would be fair to say that some Archers find commitment very difficult but, to give them their due, when they do fall in love they make caring, ardent, passionate and dependable partners, always ready to see the funny side of life and never letting problems get them down too much. What's more, because they are so cheerful, so optimistic and enthusiastic, they have a knack of buoying-up their partners' spirits.

In marriage, the Sagittarian will look for a meeting of minds. It is important for their spouse to have tolerant views, be understanding of the Archer's need for personal freedom and be prepared to put up with their casual and relaxed attitude to housework.

CHARACTER FAULTS

Sagittarians are notorious for their tactlessness. It is true that they are out-spoken and as honest as the live-long day, but their honesty can be delivered in too blunt a fashion, and they can easily wound anyone who is shy and sensitive. With them, a spade is a spade and their attitude when it comes to telling the truth or giving their opinion is: if you can't take the heat, get out of the kitchen.

Untidiness is one of the Sagittarian's worst characteristics. They simply can't understand why so much time and fuss has to be lavished on housework when there are so many more exciting things to do in life. Consequently, their homes will always have a 'lived-in' look, unless, that is, their partners like tidying-up or are pretty nifty with a cloth and some polish!

The restlessness and dislike of responsibility amongst many of these subjects might also be considered a negative character trait. Indeed, many Sagittarians actively run away from what they believe to be the shackles of marriage, positively avoiding the burden of children, the millstone of a mortgage around their necks.

HOW TO SPOT YOUR SAGITTARIAN LOVER

Sagittarians have a warm, friendly, open and sociable approach. In stature, they may be given away by their big hips and stocky thighs. Some are said to have a horsey look to their faces whilst others may be detected from afar by a neighing quality to their laugh. Male Sagittarians often go bald prematurely at the temples.

They are very casual in their dress, usually preferring to wear comfortable, informal clothes. One of their great delights is rummaging about in charity shops or jumble sales, putting together their lucky finds with such flair that the results are often surprisingly stunning.

Purples, violets, lavender and blue are the Sagittarian colours and topaz their favourite stone. Perfumes should match their sporty, easy-going character.

OTHER LOVERS WHO SHARE THE SIGN

Jenny Agutter
Woody Allen
Dame Peggy Ashcroft
Lionel Blair
Ian Botham
Ronnie Corbett
Judi Dench
Noel Edmonds
Uri Geller

Jonathan King
Chris Evert Lloyd
Paul Nicholas
Robert Robinson
Brough Scott
Steven Spielberg
Gianni Versace
Ernie Wise

CAPRICORN

22 December – 20 January

Symbol: The Goat
Ruler: Saturn
Element: Earth

KEYNOTES TO CHARACTER

Practical, driving ambition, industrious, head for business, strong sense of duty, austere, loners, emotional coolness, mean, obsessional.

THE CAPRICORN LOVER

The first thing to understand about your Capricornian companions is that they are indefatigable hard-workers. The men of the sign are ambitious and want to get-on in the world to the point that many become workaholics.

With the women, too, personal ambition is a strong motivating force, especially if they are career-minded. And, if they aren't ambitious for themselves, they tend to put all their ambitious drive into their men-folk. Indeed, of all the signs of the Zodiac it is Capricorn wives who may well earn the title of 'the power behind the throne'.

At work, Capricornians are excellent organisers. Their managerial skills and business acumen are unsurpassed and many will be found in the world of high finance. They possess a highly developed sense of duty, so will have responsibility thrust upon them and will find themselves, through persistence, tenacity and sober perseverance, systematically climbing the ladder to the top of their profession. Which, indeed, is a good thing because, for Capricornians, success in life is important and they will apply their powers of concentration until they reach their desired goals.

Underlying all this busy endeavour is a need for material security. Position and status matter a great deal to them. It is for this reason that much of their effort will be expended towards ensuring a high standard of living for themselves and their families.

Capricorn is an earth sign so, like those born under Taurus and Virgo, their dominant features include practicality, conservatism and respectability. Ruled by Saturn, they are never flamboyant or extravagant, they are able to live very frugally and are perhaps the best housekeepers in the Zodiac, knowing how to handle their resources economically. They are always prudent and careful to put something by for that inevitable rainy day.

It is their ruler, too, that gives them their reputation for having a somewhat saturnine nature. Born with an old head on young shoulders, they go through life with a maturity that belies their years. Moreover, Capricornians are self-reliant. If they have problems, they like time to themselves to think, or work things through in their own minds. It is this characteristic that may, at times, make them appear reserved, or dubs them the loners of the Zodiac.

As lovers, they are definitely not what you might call flighty or flirtatious. Nor are they the most romantic or passionate of the twelve signs. Not for them the daring exploits of the Arian in the pursuit of his lady-love, or the extravagant banquets of the Leonine female with which she impresses her mate nor, for that matter, the smouldering ardour of the Scorpio. No, Capricorns are far more realistic and, because their generally serious attitude to life is reflected in their relationships, they are not easily swept off their feet.

When choosing a suitable mate, they will aim high, for in relationships, as in all other aspects of life, they are status-seekers and have extremely high standards. In marriage, they will seek security more than passion, so will look for someone who is solid and reliable, who will shore-up their own interests, and who will work shoulder-to-shoulder in the pursuit of material stability.

Though they may not necessarily be emotionally demonstrative, they are stable and reliable, and when they do find their ideal partner they prove themselves to be very faithful, devoted and loyal. In fact, in marriage, loyalty is the most important element to Capricornians, both in terms of giving total and complete loyalty to their spouses, and in expecting total and complete loyalty in return.

So, if you're looking for a solid, steady, reliable, albeit conservative, partner in life, someone who though at times romantically undemonstrative, is nevertheless thoroughly dependable, who will provide a stable and secure home and who won't let you down in a crisis, then you don't need to look any further than the tenth sign of the Zodiac, for Capricorn is tailor-made for you.

CHARACTER FAULTS

The Capricornian ability to handle their affairs efficiently and economically can, in some, develop into parsimony. And their love of money, seeing their wealth build and grow in front of their very eyes, has given some natives of this sign a reputation for avariciousness and miserliness.

That they are formidably persistent in the attainment of their goals is a positive characteristic, but it is a trait that can all too easily flip into its negative pole when the ambition develops into an obsessional, megalomaniac pursuit of power and empire-building.

HOW TO SPOT YOUR CAPRICORN LOVER

Capricorns are often tall and thin and have a boney frame. Their faces are generally long and thin, topped by high foreheads that can be heavily lined. The features are gaunt and a rather long chin can all too often be a Capricornian tell-tale characteristic. They often look much older than they actually are, presenting a serious aspect and, unless encouraged as youngsters, many have a tendency not to laugh enough, appearing more sombre or solemn than need be.

They may dress in a rather severe fashion, usually very conventional and clean-cut. The black cocktail dress or pin-stripe suit and bowler hat are often hall-marks of those born under this sign.

Grey, black and olive green are Capricornian colours, and onyx, jet and obsidian their birthstones. Like their clothes, their perfumes have clean-cut fragrances, and the more traditional the better.

OTHER LOVERS WHO SHARE THE SIGN

HRH Princess Alexandra
Antony Andrews
Michael Aspel
Rowan Atkinson
Joan Baez
David Bellamy
Peter Barkworth
Richard Briers
Kenny Everett
Frederico Fellini

Liza Goddard
Anthony Hopkins
HRH Princess Michael of Kent
Sarah Miles
Richard Nixon
Des O'Connor
Victoria Principal
John Thaw
Cliff Thorburn

AQUARIUS

21 January – 18 February

Symbol: The Waterbearer
Ruler: Uranus
Element: Air

KEYNOTES TO CHARACTER

Loyal, altruistic, democratic, ahead of their time, head for science, eccentric, rebellious, a mind of their own.

THE AQUARIAN LOVER

The individualists of the Zodiac, Aquarians are the most unorthodox and unconventional people one is likely to meet. They purposefully avoid being pigeon-holed or categorized by following their own fashion, their own ideas and forging their own path in life. They are not the sort to join clubs and societies, preferring every time to go it alone, to do their own thing without being dictated to by others. True non-conformists, many an Aquarian goes through a rebellious, anti-Establishment period in youth and, though they do learn the art of compromise as they grow older, it is a streak in their character that never quite disappears.

Governed by the planet Uranus, they possess a mentality that can be light years ahead of their time, and it comes as no surprise that many scientists and inventors number amongst the natives of this sign. Many are what might be called 'far-sighted' and may pursue a way of life that could well be considered cranky at the time but which, actually, is simply a decade or two in advance of the current trends.

For example, many Aquarians believed in alternative lifestyles, becoming vegetarians and following a health and fitness regime, long before jogging and health-food stores became fashionable and when such beliefs and behaviour were considered quite eccentric.

In fact, nothing suits Aquarians more than being labelled eccentric. Indeed, one sometimes gets the feeling they go out of their way to be different. Some might see this as plain awkwardness or cussedness, for, usually, Aquarians can be as stubborn as mules when they want to.

Strong humanitarian ideals rule this sign. Tolerant and broadminded, Aquarians have a great respect for other people's views and beliefs. Democracy, one feels, must surely have been invented by an Aquarian. They believe in freedom of speech and the inviolability of human rights, and are always ready to take up a cause, to champion the under-dog, to campaign against cruelty and injustice to both man and beast. Where there is a cause, where there is a mission, where there is a need, wherever help is required, there will be an Aquarian to give generously and unstintingly of their service. Service to humanity is the Aquarian catch-phrase.

Though their symbol is the Water-bearer, their element, in fact, is Air. So, like the other two signs in this triplicity, Gemini and Libra, there is a certain coolness and aloofness about Aquarians when it comes to personal relationships. Morever, they are not senti-mental and certainly not given to gooey demonstrations of emotion. Nor are they overly expressive of their affections, for in general they don't like to show their feelings and are not especially good at handling emotion, whether it's their own or that of their partner.

In a relationship with an Aquarian, friendship and the exchange of ideas and viewpoints are far more impor-tant than sex. That's why they make such wonderful friends to members of both sexes. It is because of their coolness and love of independence that passion is not especially associated with this sign, yet they are caring and understanding lovers who treat their partners as equals.

In choosing a marriage partner, Aquarians can be rather idealistic. Ladies of the sign spend a great deal of time looking for the perfect chivalrous knight, whilst the gentlemen would be quite satisfied with a perfect androgenous female. Love and sex really come quite low on their list of priorities. It is perhaps for these reasons that many don't marry until later in life, some leaving it well into their middle-age.

When they do marry they are faithful, honest and loyal partners, highly inventive and with a strong element of unpredictability about them that gives their marriage a certain *'je ne sais quoi'*. It is this hint of the unexpected that gives the Aquarian partner a touch of mystery that will always be preserved and maintained within their relationships. There will, too, be that hint of cool detachment and that need for independence that means you feel you've never quite got a grip on your elusive Aquarian. But if you do want to keep a hold of one, you will need to give plenty of space, and learn to cultivate a mystique of your own to keep them guessing and intrigued about you for ever.

CHARACTER FAULTS

One of the major difficulties that Aquarians experience is an inability to express their emotions. It is this which can lead to problems in their relationships unless they are lucky enough to team-up with someone who completely understands their quirkiness.

Their need to help others, whilst laudable in itself can, for some, turn them into zealots, fanatical in their beliefs. Moreover, believing themselves to be right can develop into arrogance, which can be compounded by their stubborness.

Though far-sighted, their unconventional and unorthodox mentality may, in some, veer from the purely eccentric to the rebellious and even revolutionary. They can be intensely critical of others, especially those with entrenched conservative viewpoints, which can lead them to actively 'cock-a-snook' at the Establishment and, almost perversely, flout as many conventions as they can find.

HOW TO SPOT YOUR AQUARIAN LOVER

Aquarians may be difficult to recognise as first glance as they do not have any strong, distinguishing features, but they do possess good-looking, animated faces with clear complexions over a strong facial bone structure, and they often have thick hair. There's something about their general manner that makes them seem a lot older and more mature than they really are.

Their far-sightedness usually compels them to be in the fore-front of fashion when young, but as they mature they tend to get a little staid in their tastes. Their stubborness, too, can make them the fashion eccentrics of the Zodiac.

Turquoise, deep blue and deep yellow are colours associated with the Aquarian. The birthstones are amethyst and garnet. There is no one perfume type associated with them but once their minds have been made up they are likely to stick to one fragrance as their own favourite for evermore.

OTHER LOVERS WHO SHARE THE SIGN

Buzz Aldrin
Yasser Arafat
Michael Bentine
Claire Bloom
Ernest Borgnine
Dora Bryan
Neil Diamond
Bamber Gascoigne
Russell Grant
Germaine Greer
Benny Hill
Barry Humphries
David Jason
John McEnroe
Julia McKenzie
Frank Muir
Yoko Ono
Mary Quant
Claire Rayner
Vanessa Redgrave
Martin Shaw
Telly Savalas
Tom Selleck
David Vine

PISCES

19 February – 21 March

Symbol: The Fishes
Ruler: Neptune
Element: Water

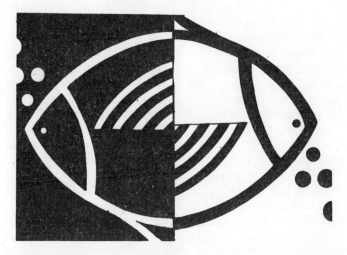

KEYNOTES TO CHARACTER

Sensitive, sympathetic, selfless, intuitive, giving, impressionable, passive, mystical, pessimistic, vague, lack of self-confidence, weak-willed, a bit of a wet-blanket.

THE PISCEAN LOVER

People born with the sun in Pisces are the least arrogant members of the Zodiac. Shy, diffident, modest, they are unlikely to push themselves forward in the way that a brash Arian might, or take centre-stage like Leo. Because of this mild manner and non-competitive attitude, they often find themselves pushed out of the spotlight and nudged into the wings by their more forceful and vociferous companions.

Pisceans are extremely sensitive creatures, mainly because they tend to let their emotions dominate their lives. They are dreamy and romantic, living very much in their own imagination and creating a fantasy world around themselves. Their idealistic (and often unrealistic) view of life, of love and relationships is sustained by the rose-coloured spectacles they like to wear and through which they see knights in shining armour, fair damsels in distress, roses around the cottage door. For it is by wearing these specs that they can soften the harsher realities around them and at the same time effectively blind themselves to any truth they cannot face.

And this, indeed, is an important side to suggestible Pisceans who can be so easily influenced by more unscrupulous characters that even when the truth stares them in the eye, they will still delude themselves and steadfastly refuse to acknowledge that they are being taken for a ride. For they do seem to prefer sticking with a difficult relationship, no matter how painful to themselves, rather than 'rocking the boat', 'making waves' (to use Piscean terminology) or generally hurting other people's feelings.

Indeed, many of these gentle natives of the twelfth sign create their own problems by making themselves into martyrs, actively laying themselves down as victims at the feet of those who are stronger or bolder than themselves. No wonder, then, that so many Pisceans are taken advantage of, and no wonder, too, that so many then lament their fates and end up feeling very sorry for themselves.

As friends, they are warm and receptive and make wonderfully-caring lovers. They have an inexhaustible supply of understanding and their compassion seemingly knows no bounds. As partners, they are kind and sensitive, loving, sympathetic and always ready to help. Moreover, because they are so intuitive, they are instinctively able to sense the mood of their spouses and readily empathise with their feelings and their needs.

Both males and females of the sign are sentimental, clinging types. In marriage they are extremely devoted and supportive partners. Female Pisceans exude a feminine fragility and are vulnerable creatures, so need to feel that their husbands will protect them. When she does find her Mr Right, someone who is tender and understanding, Ms Pisces will do all she can to please him.

Mr Pisces makes a considerate husband, generous with his time, his money and his affection. In fact, giving has to be the most important aspect in the relationship because the Piscean simply loves to share every experience, every feeling, every part of his or her being.

Within a relationship it is love and not sex that is important because, again, it is the element of giving and sharing and the intimate rapport of mutual understanding which two lovers develop together that turns-on the Piscean. In fact, sex simply for its own sake without tenderness or romance is quite a turn off for them.

If you settle for a Piscean you will have the good fortune to share in a richly spiritual life, deeply loving, and caring of humanity and the environment. Moreover, because many Pisceans are artistically gifted or musically accomplished your home is likely to be a centre of creativity – peaceful, nostalgic, romantic, spiritually inspiring and always warm and welcoming.

CHARACTER FAULTS

Pisces belongs to the Water element and it would indeed be fair to say that many of its natives have a tendency to be a bit wet. Emotionally they can sometimes go a little over the top, plunging-in out of their depth because they allow themselves to be ruled by their feelings rather than working things out logically. Because of this trait they can somewhat drift through life, swimming about aimlessly without any positive aim or direction, latching on to people and situations as they crop up.

And being water creatures, they seem to lack a firm hold on *terra firma*, often unable to get to grips with the realities of life, with the nitty-gritty of everyday living. Though creatures of the deep, they do, nevertheless, seem to spend a lot of their lives with their heads in the clouds.

Some Pisceans take a gloomy view of life. Unable to cope with harsh realities, some develop a habit of escaping either into their own fantasy worlds or by taking drugs and alcohol. Also, there may be a tendency to emotional instability or depression as many are prone to moodiness or sulking.

Though the majority are warm and loving, it should not be forgotten that there are a few who, like their symbol, the Fish, can be slippery customers, thoroughly cold-blooded and ruthless.

HOW TO SPOT YOUR PISCEAN LOVER

You'll be able to spot your Piscean heart-throb miles away by their sensitively expressive faces. It is the eyes which are their most prominent features, mostly soft, watery and limpid and often light in colour – greeny blue, delicate grey or violet.

Piscean feet are EITHER tiny and nimble as any dancer OR, large and clumsy, constantly in the way or simply tripping over themselves. Indeed, many Pisceans are prone to a variety of foot-troubles.

Fashion-wise, Piscean ladies look wonderful in natural

fibres. They have a delicate sense of dress, and somehow always know how to look different. They amass classical items, which on them never seem to date as they are worn in such a way as to achieve a look which is quite original and which stands in a class of its own.

Sea green, purple and rich blues are Piscean colours. Crystal, moonstones and emeralds are associated with the sign. Perfumes that are preferred are delicate, floral fragrances that leave their whisper in the air as this lady passes by.

OTHER LOVERS WHO SHARE THE SIGN

Joss Ackland
HRH The Duke of York
Terence Brady
Jasper Carrott
Jilly Cooper
Tyne Daly
HRH Prince Edward
Bruce Forsyth
Jools Holland

Frankie Howerd
HRH The Duchess of Kent
Paul Jones
Leo McKern
Patrick Moore
Elizabeth Taylor
Julie Walters
Dennis Waterman

ARE YOU COMPATIBLE?

No astrologer worth their salt would make predictions on the compatibility of two people simply by looking at their sun sign alone. Indeed, for every rule that might be laid down on sun sign compatibility there will be at the very least half a dozen couples ready to disprove it.

This is because each individual is influenced and affected by all the planets in different ways, to a greater or lesser degree. No two Taureans will be found to be exactly alike because the position of the planets at their time of birth would form a different pattern, and so affect each in a different way. One Taurean might be wildly attracted to a Leo, let's say, whilst another Taurean might find that same Leo a total turn-off.

In order to properly make any prediction on whether two people are compatible or not, an astrologer would have to erect a birth chart for each person, using the exact time, date and location of birth. This plots the planets in their astrological houses and gives a very clear picture of the character and personality, drives and motivation, aims and ambitions, likes and dislikes, likely health, wealth and life trends that will potentially affect that individual.

One birth chart is then mapped onto the other so points of similarity and discord become obvious. In this way, it is possible to make predictions about the areas of agreement and disagreement that the couple is likely to come across in their lives together. If there are enough points of agreement, enough love, understanding and tolerance between the two, their relationship is likely to be a success, whether their sun signs are overtly compatible or not.

To erect a birth chart correctly obviously takes time and a good deal of experience, but is worthwhile if two people really want to understand themselves and their relationship more intimately. However, there are some pointers which can be used as a rule-of-thumb guide and which will give some fairly elementary clues as to whether two people are likely to get on well together, or whether they are more likely to clash.

Astrology tells us that there are certain signs which, on the whole, are known to go well together because they belong to the same ELEMENT group. The twelve signs of the Zodiac are divided into four ELEMENTS, and each one contains three signs, all of which share similar characteristics. Therefore people belonging to these signs have a similar outlook on life.

The four elements are EARTH, AIR, FIRE and WATER and the three signs belonging to each category are listed thus:–

EARTH	AIR	FIRE	WATER
Taurus	Gemini	Aries	Cancer
Virgo	Libra	Leo	Scorpio
Capricorn	Aquarius	Sagittarius	Pisces

The EARTH group is categorised as 'physical' because people belonging to it are generally practical, solid, hard-working and materialistic.

The AIR group is characterised as 'intellectual' for these people have lively minds and are interested in communication. FIRE is the so-called 'spiritual' group and these folk are active, enthusiastic, creative and philosophical. WATER is the 'emotional' element and those born in this category are sympathetic, impressionable and deeply sensitive.

EARTH

People belonging to the EARTH group may be described as down-to-earth or as having their feet firmly planted on *terra firma*. In the main, trustworthy and reliable, they are solid, practical, level-headed individuals, who are strongly aware of their responsibilities. On the negative side, they can be somewhat stolid and doggedly persistent. Although this can prove to their advantage at times, at other times they can be infuriatingly stubborn.

Money and material well-being matters a great deal to the EARTH types, and they are prepared to work hard to achieve their ambitions and goals in life. All those born under the three EARTH signs are careful and cautious and thus in their own inimitable way tend not to rush head-long into relationships or affairs of the heart without having prepared the ground first. Therefore, marriages between the EARTH signs tend to be stable and in general would seem durable and long lasting.

AIR

Those belonging to the category AIR may be described primarily as communicators. The signs belonging to the AIR group are considered 'intellectual', that is, they deal very much in the realm of ideas. In partnerships, then, people born with their sun in Gemini, Libra and Aquarius tend to look for a companion who is like-minded, will be intellectually stimulating, and will share their interests and ideas. To them, this coming together of mutual minds is more important than sexual or romantic compatibility.

However, although many are bright, alert and seemingly intelligent, because of their vast appetite for picking up information, their knowledge will often be found to be merely skin-deep. It also appears that they are much better at generating and exchanging ideas than actually putting them into practice. This characteristic may be somewhat disconcerting to other, more productive or practically-oriented signs, which is why others within the same element group are more likely to make understanding and sympathetic partners.

AIR types are not over emotional and may not particularly be described as passionate because, on the whole, there is a certain coolness and aloofness about them. As with their wide-ranging tastes in interests and spare-time pursuits, they equally like variety in their relationships too. Hence, many belonging to this category tend to be flirtatious, immensely enjoying the thrill that new relationships can bring.

The superficiality that can be shown towards their interests may also be reflected in their attitudes to long-term relationships. Many are afraid of serious commitment and consequently either shy away from marriage or tend to divorce and marry more than once. Many ideal marriages between two AIR types either spring from, or develop into successful business partnerships.

FIRE

People belonging to the FIRE element are fiery types. Emotionally they are passionate and their love burns with an ardent intensity. Lively and enthusiastic, those born with their suns in Aries, Leo and Sagittarius, pursue their relationships and love affairs with energy and excitement.

Warm-hearted and exuberant, they have magnetic characters and exude a goodly amount of sex appeal. Easily able to influence others, they spread their sunshine wherever they go. Indeed, their optimism is so infectious that people with whom they come into contact can't help but be swept along on the wave of their enthusiasm.

Love is extremely important to them. In fact, life without love for a FIRE sign is a very dull life indeed. In love they can be consumed by their emotions, totally enraptured by the partner they are with. But they can also be experimental and flirtatious, often trying several relationships before finally committing themselves seriously to one partner.

WATER

People belonging to the WATER signs of Cancer, Scorpio and Pisces are characterised as sensitive and deeply emotional. Indeed, when it comes to the emotions, they may quite justifiably be described as intense.

WATER people can be complex individuals, mainly because they seem to be driven by their feelings rather than their reason. Often misunderstood and easily hurt (by what appears to others as apparently trivial slights), they counteract any emotional bruising by metaphorically retiring to quietly lick their wounds in a safe corner, on their own. Thus they are considered moody, outgoing one minute and seemingly sullen the next.

Partners of WATER types, then, have to tread carefully around these people's sensitivities lest they inadvertently upset them.

Another characteristic of the WATER element group is impressionability. They are so easily influenced, persuaded first one way and then another that they may be considered somewhat gullible, falling for any hard-luck story that comes along. Many have made poor marriages precisely for this reason.

In a relationship with a native of one of the more dominant elements, such as FIRE, for example, the WATER individual may be quite literally thought of as wet, or as a bit of a drip. In such circumstances these individuals may well resort to playing emotional games which could adversely affect the partnership. But, in a more balanced relationship, these natives of the WATER element can be immensely caring and sympathetic. In this situation they make extremely loving, understanding and generous partners.

COMBINATIONS

Although there are no hard and fast rules about who gets on with whom, signs within the same element group tend to think and feel in similar ways. However, do remember that much depends on individual make-up as to how two people will react and interact with each other. Besides, attraction of opposites can work extremely well – even if sometimes sparks do fly! So when you are assessing how you and your partner fare according to your element, consider first how those elements would combine in their natural state and then apply this to your own relationship.

For example, if you were born in the sign of Pisces you belong to the WATER element. If your lover is a Cancerian you are probably well-matched, temperamentally at least, because he belongs to the same element as you do. If your latest heart-throb is a Leo, though, there may be a lot of fizz in your relationship but, because he belongs to the element FIRE, there may be times when your relationship swings from steamy passion, at the heights, to a bit of a damp squib, on a bad day.

EARTH & EARTH

ELEMENT COMBINATION

Earth – the Mother from which all vegetation grows. From within her comes life, with her we can build our shelters and find protection and security. She provides stability and a sense of permanence. But alone, without the other elements, she can become barren and sterile.

RELATIONSHIP

A partnership characterised by physical activity and hard work. Both need structure and routine but are thoroughly dependable and reliable. A strong relationship which is likely to last but which might be thought of as somewhat stolid and unimaginative. This makes a fairly materialistic partnership with a strong need for both financial and domestic security. Both are ambitious and highly achievement-motivated, especially so Capricorn men. Together they can become plodding, set in their ways and even somewhat old-fashioned.

EARTH & AIR

ELEMENT COMBINATION

Gentle wind can help to pollinate earth's flowers and trees. Air can dry-up the earth. High Winds can whip up earth bringing destruction and mayhem.

RELATIONSHIP

This relationship could be very beneficial to both parties although it can have its difficulties. It can work if each is tolerant of the other and accepts the partner's differences of opinion. At worst, EARTH can be a little too stolid for excitable AIR. AIR can be too volatile for steady, practical EARTH. Down-to-earth Taurus, for example, can smother and restrain Aquarius' need for free-expression whilst Gemini's airy-fairy attitude to life can irritate and completely dry-out long-suffering, practical Virgoan's patience.

EARTH & FIRE

ELEMENT COMBINATION

Earth cannot yield her bounty without the gentle heat of the sun. Too much heat can scorch the earth. Earth can smother a fire.

RELATIONSHIP

At its best the relationship can be warm, productive and constructive. The EARTH characters are solid and stable and can provide the right environment for bringing to fruition the lively ideas of their FIERY partners. At worst, EARTH can become scorched by over-passionate FIRE, whilst plodding EARTH can smother FIRE'S enthusiasm for life. An over-ardent Aries male, for example, can overwhelm the more placid Virgoan lady whilst the more plodding Taurean can completely dull the spontaneity and excitement of, say, a Sagittarian partner.

EARTH & WATER

ELEMENT COMBINATION

Without water, the earth's plants wither and die. Water refreshes earth and earth provides a container in which to channel water's energies. Earth can constrain water, trapping it in until it becomes foetid. Drip by drip, water can wear earth away. Too much water makes earth boggy and unproductive.

RELATIONSHIP

This relationship can be refreshing, powerful and life-giving. It can be one of the most mutually helpful combinations of all the cross elements. EARTH can help channel WATER'S inspirational ideas and WATER can refresh EARTH'S more stolid nature. Of the WATER signs, Scorpio is the strongest, portraying the torrential side of this element, and can make a formidable partner for the gentler Virgoans or Taureans.

On the negative side, WATER can swamp EARTH and materialistic EARTH can tread on WATER'S sensitivity. A soggy Cancerian, for instance, can weigh down a Capricornian or Virgoan partner, whilst making these even more plodding, and slowing down their constructive urge. On the other hand, Taurean's big feet can trample all over Piscean's delicate sensibilities without even realising it.

AIR & AIR

ELEMENT COMBINATION

Oxygen fills our lungs, breezes fan the flames, gasses burn to give us power and heat, winds whip up tornado and typhoon. Air in all its different guises – always on the move, never still.

RELATIONSHIP

AIR couples enjoy all forms of movement and communications. They thrive on variety and love new ideas and gadgets. Together, two AIR people would find great intellectual stimulation in each other. But these people need a sense of freedom in their lives so their relationships must be fluid, tolerant and flexible. Talking, discussing and debating together is a must for these two, although often this can be simply empty, superficial 'hot air', where the spirit is willing but the flesh is weak. In close relationships they may appear cool and distant, and, the men in particular, often seem afraid of total commitment. The question that may be asked about this relationship is: how long will it take to blow itself out?

AIR & FIRE

ELEMENT COMBINATION

A gentle breeze can bring soothing relief on a scorching day. Air can fan the embers into flame. Volatile, so mixed in the wrong proportions, these two can become combustible!

RELATIONSHIP

A potentially good and compatible relationship – stimulating, breezy and exciting. FIRE and AIR both share enthusiasm, a love for excitement and an enjoyment of stimulating ideas. Sagittarian's bubbly vivaciousness, for instance, can be quite inspirational to

Libra's creative ideas. Gemini's versatile and flexible nature can be just the right spur for the impulsiveness of an Aries partner. On the minus side, AIR may cool FIRE'S ardour and, at worst, AIR and FIRE together can become volatile – a combustible mixture!

AIR & WATER

ELEMENT COMBINATION

Water and air are both essential to life. Together they can produce clouds, damp mists, rain and tempests. Whipped up they make stimulating, refreshing bubbles but also superficial froth.

RELATIONSHIP

Although individually AIR and WATER are both essential for life, there are times when together they can prove a somewhat stormy and tempestuous partnership. On the other hand, this relationship can be bubbly, frothy, and full of fun. When it isn't going so well, though, WATER can dampen AIR'S buoyant and lively spirits, and AIR can whip WATER into a lather! Pisces and Cancer, can be too clinging for the independent nature of a Gemini or Aquarian partner. And the bright and breezy, aloof and non-committal attitude of a Libran, for example, may not have enough substance to satisfy a Scorpio's depth of feeling and need for a secure base.

FIRE & FIRE

ELEMENT COMBINATION

Fire provides gentle heat, light and power. Fire uncontrolled can burn, consuming all that stands in its way, reducing both beauty and ugliness indiscriminately to dust and ashes.

RELATIONSHIP

Together, two FIRE people make an energetic and enthusiastic couple. Physically warm and outgoing, they make an open, friendly and generous pair. Thrusting and positive, they are born leaders so each may try to get the upper hand over the other. A FIRE individual is passionate, but sometimes can get carried away in the heat of the moment. Literally, fiery of temperament, this is a wonderfully exciting relationship, but will the passion be all-consuming? And then, having consumed, will it burn itself out?

FIRE & WATER

ELEMENT COMBINATION

When the temperature is right, fire and water combined produce steam power. Too much, and the water will evaporate away. A bucket of water will instantly douse a fire.

RELATIONSHIP

A tricky relationship although at the right temperature these two make a powerful combination. Turn up the heat and WATER boils away. But WATER can douse FIRE'S passion and enthusiasm. Scorpio, with its own smouldering passion and intensity is perhaps the happiest with a FIRE partner but Cancer and Pisces will find themselves heated to boiling point by the noisy, forcefulness and intolerance of the Aries, Leo or Sagittarian. In their turn, the fiery three may feel that a Cancer, Scorpio or Piscean partner can pour buckets of water over their emotional ardour, repress their verve for living by throwing a wet blanket over their heads.

WATER & WATER

ELEMENT COMBINATION

Water is a basic requisite of living things. Gentle, soothing and refreshing water can give life but, equally, too much water can destroy life. High seas and floods can swamp land, can drown livestock, can destroy entire populations.

RELATIONSHIP

A sensitive and emotional pair with plenty of soul and much empathy and feeling for each other. Each will have great depth of feeling and so will readily empathise with his or her partner and also with others in their circle. These people are characterised by their caring natures. For example, Cancerians of both sexes are particularly home-loving and enjoy making a warm nest for their partners and families. Generally, all three WATER signs of Cancer, Scorpio and Pisces are impressionable. Also they all love peace and domestic harmony so much that they tend to go with the tide, always willing to please their partner.

With these two there is plenty of idealism, but, on the

negative side, when together they can be extremely 'wet' with a serious lack of worldliness and a lack of the drive and initiative that is so necessary to tackle the nitty-gritty tasks of everyday life.

Cross-matching your element groupings in this way will give a pretty good idea of the sort of relationship you are likely to establish together. But remember, just because it might be suggested here that your sign may clash with that of your lover, it doesn't mean you should start filing for divorce! It simply means that there are areas of discord but that those differences, once recognised, could be worked on and overcome.

HOW TO COURT YOUR LOVER

Part of loving another person is wanting to please them, getting a thrill from buying just the right present, knowing what turns them on, what brings a smile to the lips or a tear to the eye.

Sometimes, especially during the early stages of a relationship, you may not be very sure of your new lover's tastes, or you may have an occasion when you need to impress them (or their parents!), or simply want to get to know that special person in your life just that little bit better, find out their likes and dislikes, their preferences or potential.

Knowing your lover's date of birth will at the very least give you a way in. And though not everyone will conform one hundred percent to their sign, we do know, after thousands of years of astrological observation, that people born under one sign are influenced and affected in different ways to those born under another. However, those born within the same sign, by and large, tend to show similar tastes, similar inclinations and similar predilections.

Each sign of the Zodiac is associated with lucky colours and stones so you'll be able to buy your lover that special sweater in just the right shade, or choose the engagement ring that's not only a symbol of your love, but that will bring good fortune as well. You will also know the type of entertainment, flowers, toys and gadgets that would please, how to impress, wine, dine them and woo them in style.

ARIES

PRESENTS

When considering what to give an Arian for Christmas or for a birthday present, put together all the elements that are associated with the sign. Firstly, they are active people so will appreciate anything instant, immediate, sporty perhaps. Don't buy them a kit of any sort because they would be too impatient to spend time knitting a jumper, let's say; even doing a puzzle is too time-consuming for them. So, go for something like tennis racquets or a rowing machine. Membership of the local fitness club or sports centre would also please. Or perhaps something to do with camping, such as a Swiss army knife, or a new, bright-coloured ruck-sack.

Secondly, they belong to the Fire element so if it's Christmas you could give a special, scented candle and, if you can afford it, a beautiful candle-holder, which would grace their table or elegantly sit on their mantlepiece.

Thirdly, this sign rules the head so, for her, you might consider a silk head-scarf, or an appointment at the best hairdressing salon in town. And beautiful expensive golden earrings would always give great delight. For Mr Aries, a fedora, perhaps.

Diamonds and rubies come under the rulership of this sign so if you want to surprise her with a knock-out engagement ring, go for a cluster of these two stones.

If you're thinking about buying your Arian lover some clothes then think RED. This is the Arian colour – how about an irresistible red shirt for him or a sumptuous red angora sweater for her.

HOLIDAYS

Activity holidays will spark romance for the Arian subject. They hate conventional, organized holidays – a package-deal to Benidorm is anathema for these folk. They need adventure, excitement, the thrill of discovery, of exploring and forging new pathways. Sleeping under the stars, hacking through the jungles of South America, trekking overland to Samarkand, these are the sorts of holidays that will inspire natives of this sign. Taking up an action sport, too, will be a thrill – para-gliding, shooting the rapids in a canoe or joining a group of mountain-climbers tackling the Matterhorn.

TAURUS

PRESENTS

Taureans adore beautiful things so there shouldn't be too much difficulty when it comes to choosing that all-important gift for them. As important as the present, however, is the way it is wrapped, so do take special care in the presentation of your gift. Choose glossy, metallic paper and add a golden bow, or wrap it in a dainty, pastel, floral print then tie it in delicate ribbon to set it off to perfection.

Taureans belong to the element Earth so anything to do with their gardens will be most appreciated. The latest book on clematis, perhaps, some gardening gloves or vouchers from the local garden centre. Seeds, plants, rose-bushes, trees, would all be loved. And have you thought about a Bonsai kit perhaps? Or better still a garden trug which she, dressed in a flowing gown of lace, will use on a scented summer's morning when she picks her flowers, dreamily laying each bloom in her basket, for all the world like one of those hapless heroines of the eighteenth century so romantically portrayed in the 1930's movies.

Their earthiness may be approached in another way, when it comes to buying presents for them, and that is through their appetites. Taureans love food, and may have a sweet tooth, so will always appreciate luxurious chocolates or a bottle of a fine liqueur. A bottle of port and a pot of Stilton would make his eyes light up.

Taurus rules the throat, so scarves and pretty lace collars would suit female Taureans. And jewellery, of course, to grace her throat. Choose a necklace made of beaten copper, or lapis lazuli or jade. Delicately-worked coral, too, is appropriate for Taureans. And if it's an engagement ring you have in mind, then it has to be emerald, the Taurean stone. He would be delighted with a luxurious cashmere polo-neck sweater, a carefully-chosen tie, or perhaps a jaunty silk cravat.

When you're buying her clothes, head towards the gentle pastel colours: Madonna blue should especially enhance her complexion. Creams, light green and pink are all equally associated with this sign.

HOLIDAYS

Luxury and comfort will be the prerequisite require-ment of any holiday for a Taurean. If there is the slightest hint of discomfort, of having to rough it, even for one night, you can forget the whole thing. They will spend a lot of time and money on careful plans, making arrangements just so, getting their holiday wardrobe right. Indeed clothes play such a large part in the holiday, judging from the preparations beforehand, that if several trips to the glossy stores, along Fifth Avenue, perhaps, or the Champs-Elysées, could be arranged, so much the better.

Taureans love beauty so spending time looking at art treasures, museums and galleries will please them enormously.

GEMINI

PRESENTS

There is never any reason to be stumped over what to buy a Geminian, for they have such wide interests. But if you're really stuck, think of their most salient characteristic – their love of anything to do with communication.

Something, then, connected with writing and reading will please them greatly. Gold-plated pens, beautiful, personalized stationery, even a word-processor if your budget can stretch to it! A Filofax would be just up their street, and what about a portable telephone or one for the car? Foreign language books, language tapes and records would go down well, especially if the language was of the country to be visited on the next holiday. Books, books and even more books are always a delight to the Geminian. Games, too, to satisfy their sense of fun and competitive razor-sharp mentality and wit.

Gemini rules the hands, which gives a wide brief, from gloves to manicure sets, from costume jewellery to a book on hand analysis. Talking of jewellery, if you have a special engagement ring in mind, there are several suitable stones associated with this sign. Peridot, beryl, chrysolite, agate and diamond all come under the aegis of Gemini.

If you're thinking about something for the man in your life then the hands, again, may give some inspiration. Anything connected with tools, or with D.I.Y. would suit. Or, why not start him off on yet another hobby? Find a craft kit, paper-making, perhaps, or buy him a stunt kite, or better still, a model aeroplane.

The intellectual colour, yellow, is associated with Gemini, and so are silver and white. If buying items of clothing for your heart-throb, do bear these special colours in mind.

HOLIDAYS

Variety is the key to a happy holiday for the Geminian. They possibly have the lowest boredom threshold of the entire Zodiac and if they aren't stimulated the whole time, constantly kept on the move, going from one interest to another, the Geminian will consider their holiday a complete flop. They adore learning, discovering, finding-out, so will want to immerse themselves in new cultures, new languages, new customs. Exploration will play a large part and will assuage their burning curiosity, so historical buildings and sites of antiquity will attract them like a magnet. But perhaps because of their love of travel and their apparent insatiable need for stimulation, a touring holiday would be just the ticket for a Geminian.

CANCER

PRESENTS

Cancerians are notoriously sentimental and nostalgic people, so any presents that hark-back to the past or have a romantic appeal will be especially loved. Any little *objets d'art*, particularly if made of silver, the Cancerian metal, such as silver boxes, picture frames, rose-bowls or candelabras, will bring great pleasure to them. Still with the Cancerian metal in mind, what about a set of silver drinking goblets, or an engraved tankard for him or a silver hair-brush and comb for her?

Because they are such dedicated home-makers something special for the home will really please them too. Part of their home-making is cooking. Items to do with the kitchen would be really appreciated – a humerous apron for him, the latest gadget for chopping and mincing, a set of splendid copper pans or a barbecue; a bone china tea-cup and saucer for her, or porcelain bowls or a crystal fruit dish. If all other inspiration dries up, cookery books will never go amiss and will be treasured year after year.

The sign of Cancer rules the chest. Pearl necklaces and silver pendants would certainly grace Ms Cancer's bossom. For a really special treat, what about a silk bodice or hand-made lace lingerie? If you're taking her out for the evening, spoil her with a corsage to pin at her shoulder – white roses, lillies, honeysuckle and mimosa, all governed by this sign, would give-off a heavenly scent throughout the evening and make your partner feel like a million dollars.

Stones which come under the domain of Cancer are principally pearls. But moonstones, too, are associated with this sign as it is ruled by the Moon. So, if you're looking for that extra special present that will take her breath away, look for a lovely piece set with moonstones and just watch the delight in her face as she unwraps it.

HOLIDAYS

Holidays by the sea attract Cancerians, but in general those born under this sign look for cosy, homely comforts when considering venturing forth on holiday. Ideally, they would prefer to stay put, enjoying relaxing in their home surroundings, sun-bathing in the back garden, finding time for all the domestic little jobs they never seem to get round to during the rest of the year.

On the whole, Cancerians don't enjoy travel, it seems to upset their system – and particularly their digestion. But they're quite at home on water, so if the holiday has something to do with water sports, involves boating or sailing, or simply pottering about on the seashore, especially if the climate is pleasantly warm, they will find themselves in their true element.

LEO

PRESENTS

Leos need to feel spoilt. They love extravagant, showy presents, the more expensive the better. Never skimp when you're buying for your Leonine lover, they simply won't appreciate it. Don't forget Leo is the king of the Zodiac and as such needs to be treated as one – well, at least on their birthday.

Gold, of course, is the precious metal associated with royalty, so it's no surprise that it should come under the rulership of Leo. Anything made of gold would please, such as a gilt frame, an exquisite wafer-thin watch, a gold pen, even a small brooch or a tie-pin. But don't worry if your purse won't stretch to gold, there's a lot of beautiful costume jewellery that will be just right for them, that still looks a million dollars but doesn't actually cost a fortune.

Luxurious gifts also delight your Leo heart-throb. Soft towel!ing robes, especially if monographed, toiletries and perfumes – but make sure they're classy ones – silk stockings for her or a pure silk tie for him.

Luxury eats and drinks are also drooled over by Leos. How about making up a small hamper with all their special favourites? Ply him with a good vintage bottle of wine, or warm the cockles of his heart with an old ruby port. Hand-made chocolate truffles for her or, for that really special occasion, splash-out on a bottle of champagne and drink it, ice-cold, together in a hot foaming bath!

It's worth remembering the colour gold again if you're thinking of buying clothes, but, in fact, all the colours of the sun – red and yellow, burnished gold, rich oranges – would suit a Leo. And choose sumptuous fabrics like silks and satins, velvets and brocades. Fur, of course, would be right for a Leo and nowadays there are some beautiful imitation furs that won't cost the earth or offend sensibilities yet will appeal to their animal instincts.

The important thing to remember is that there is nothing stingy about Leos – they will lavish those they love with extravagance and no thought of expense. But they will expect the same generosity back.

Rubies, amber and topaz are the stones associated with this sign so the Leo girl of your dreams would go a bundle on a ruby engagement ring set into a band of burnished gold.

HOLIDAYS

When Leos go on holiday they want the best. First-class travel, luxury, caviar and champagne all the way! As in every other aspect of their lives, Leos need to be made to feel special, need to be the centre of attraction. If their finances give them a choice between a two-week package-deal holiday in the sun or a week-end in a five-star hotel, it would be the latter that Leos would choose without a shadow of a doubt.

VIRGO

PRESENTS

Virgoans are the neat and tidy, fussy members of the Zodiac. They are passionate about hygiene, health and nutrition, and careful about their appearance and the environment in which they live.

Belonging to the element Earth, all love flowers and plants, and many have 'green fingers'. Buy your lover some of the more exclusive seeds or unusual plants whether for indoors or for the garden. A bouquet of fresh flowers will always delight them, but so too would silk flowers or a basket of dried, autumn-tinted flowers and leaves.

With their affinity with Mother Nature, and their preoccupation with health matters, they would certainly appreciate herbal toiletries, natural soaps and shampoos. Herbal teas, especially those wrapped in pretty packages, will please them greatly, as will organic honey, nuts and dried fruits. For a special occasion, treat your Virgoan lover to an aromatherapy massage, she will adore the sensation and be putty in your arms afterwards.

For him, how about booking an appointment with a reflexologist? Marvellous if he's been under some pressure at work. And think what the de-stressing will do for your love life!

Ruled by Mercury, they can be bookish people, so will always appreciate reading matter. Books on healthy eating would be appropriate, a history of perfume, a D.I.Y. manual on pot-pourri or anything about alternative medicine.

When buying clothes or jewellery for the Virgoan lady in your life, think of autumn, both in terms of colours and the motifs associated with that time of year. Russets, rich browns and deep-golds suit them best. Think of leaf patterns, of ears of corn, of bunches of grapes. Mother Nature's cornocopia patterned on a jersey, perhaps, or a delicate gold or platinum 'horn of plenty' on a dainty chain.

Sapphire is the stone associated with Virgo, so, too, are jasper, agate and sardonyx. If you're thinking of proposing to your Virgoan lady-love, present her with a gorgeous sapphire engagement ring, but whatever you do, make sure it's neat and pretty. This lady does not appreciate loud, showy jewellery; she prefers the subtle understatement which rather characterises her nature.

HOLIDAYS

Holidays with a decided rural or horticultural setting particularly appeal to Virgoans. They enjoy staying in farm-houses, perhaps helping with the live-stock, wandering through farm estates and taking in the scenes at cattle markets and agricultural shows. Lady Virgoans like nothing better than visiting historical houses, cruising around the gardens, swapping horticultural ideas and picking up tips for when they get back to their own flower borders at home.

Farms of another sort also attract those born with the sun in Virgo – health farms. In fact, Virgoans would consider a week at a spa or health resort as the height of bliss, unwinding from the punishing schedules and heavy work-loads they impose upon themselves in their working lives.

LIBRA

PRESENTS

Whatever you give your Libran heart-throb, make sure it's wrapped elegantly. These are refined people, their tastes are sophisticated and very selective so gifts must be stylish and as exclusive as possible. Balance and harmony are their mottoes in life and they will spend a great deal of time blending and harmonizing their knick-knacks and possessions, colour co-ordinating them, getting the feel just right. Because of this, it may be difficult to choose anything for their houses or their flats, so perhaps it is best to concentrate on personal presents instead.

Aftershaves and perfumes are a good bet, but don't forget they have to appear stylish and be of excellent quality. Perhaps a delicate *art nouveau* scent bottle for the lady in your life, or for the man, a mahogany-backed clothes brush with his initials in silver.

If he's the outdoor type, he'd love a silver or pewter hip flask – again, have his initials inscribed on it in a classical font. For her, a pair of opera glasses. Music is very important to Librans and as they go to as many concerts, performances and recitals as they can, tickets are bound to be met by applause. Record and CD tokens will always be appreciated. And so, come to that, would a subscription to a favourite music magazine.

The Libran metal is copper so any jewellery fashioned out of this will be greatly loved. As far as stones go, the opal comes under the dominion of this sign. Alternatives are quartz and malachite, but if you're thinking of an engagement ring for your Libran lady you wouldn't go far wrong if you chose a sapphire set in red gold.

Pastel colours suit the Libran temperament and complexion, so if buying clothes for your paramour think of pale blues and greens and pink.

Though presents for the home may be difficult to get right, there is just one item which is appropriate to the Libran – kitchen scales. If she hasn't already been given a set, you might consider it as a gift for a first anniversay, or as a 'setting-up home together' present. But make sure that they're the traditional types with delightful brass weights – just like the ones that always represent the sign of Libra.

HOLIDAYS

Above all, Librans are attracted to peaceful settings and beautiful locations. They don't enjoy mad, energetic holidays, but prefer calm and serenity. The noisy hub-bub of a beach thronging with people is not for them, nor is the hectic pace of cramming all the sights of a country into one week-end. They choose their location carefully and, once there, they like to stay put, leaving the hustle and bustle far behind them.

What these people want out of a holiday is quiet relaxation where they can take things easily and yet be mentally stimulated. So, in their exclusive retreats they will need scintillating company. They particularly enjoy meeting new people, making new friends and exchanging ideas and philosophical thoughts – often well into the early hours.

SCORPIO

PRESENTS

Deep, secretive and moody characterises the Scorpio temperament. Ruled by Pluto, the dark mysterious planet on the very edge of our solar system, Scorpios revel in mystery and see themselves as budding detectives, always ready to solve problems and find out the answers to riddles. Books of word puzzles would keep your Scorpio lover entertained for hours. Murder mysteries, spy stories and intrigues will keep her guessing 'whodunnit'.

If your Scorpio heart-throb is academically-minded, they will be fascinated by all aspects of the workings of the mind. Psychoanalysis will be particularly intriguing, so think about a book on Freudian psychology, or the modern techniques of psycho-dynamics. Works on forensic detection, criminological case-histories or auto-biographies of outstanding military figures could also suit.

In mythology, Pluto was the ruler of the underworld and, true to the legend, many Scorpios enjoy delving into subjects that are on the fringes of orthodoxy, subjects that are known as alternative or paranormal. Buy your lover some occult paraphernalia, a pendulum for Christmas and let them try their hand at dowsing, a set of runes, perhaps, or an astrological chess-set, even a crystal ball. If these children of Pluto never use these artefacts they will enjoy them as beautiful and unusual ornaments and use them as focal points in conversation with their guests.

Leather is particularly associated with this sign. Treat your Scorpio lady-love to a beautiful Gucci handbag, or buy your male heart-throb a personal organizer. Both Ms and Mr Scorpio will go a bundle on a slim attaché case or, if the purse won't stretch to that, a simple but elegant belt will be treasured.

Stones governed by Scorpio are rubies and opals – gorgeous set into an engagement ring. The colours that best suit are black and deep, rich red.

Scorpios have a notorious reputation, for they are known as the sexiest people in the Zodiac. So, if you want to buy her something really sexy, think about a pair of French cami-knickers or a sumptuous nightdress, and lavish her with spicy, exotic perfume. Don't go for anything light and florally – it simply wouldn't have enough impact to match her strong personality.

For a sexy Scorpio man, well, buy him some black satin sheets and just let him lead you to his bedroom. . . .

HOLIDAYS

Scorpios go for interesting, unusual and out-of-the-way places, so their ideal holiday would take them to locations which might be described as off-the-beaten-track. This is mainly because there is nothing worse for these types than to find themselves surrounded by hoards of camera-clicking tourists or battalions of sight-seers grabbing for tawdry and expensive souvenirs.

As Scorpios like 'collecting' countries, they tend to go to different places every time, meticulously researching beforehand the customs, culture and way of life. Even before they set out, they have a fair idea about the country they are about to visit, and will have learnt some useful phrases that will come in very handy just at the right moment.

SAGITTARIUS

PRESENTS

Sagittarians are the globe-trotters of the Zodiac. Active, energetic and forever on the go, so if you're in a quandry about a present for your lover born under this sign, think of sportswear and accessories. Buy her a tracksuit in the Sagittarian colours of purple, pink and dark blue. Present him with a set of badminton raquets and promise faithfully you'll play a match with him every week. Because they're the sign of the Archer, what could be more appropriate than booking them in for archery lessons? That will send cupid's arrow straight to their heart!

Because he's on the hoof so much, he won't be able to plug-in to his favourite music so why not think of sounds in the saddle, as it were. Surprise him with a personal stereo and a couple of tapes to go with it, that should keep his spirits up on those early morning jogging sessions.

If it's his birthday, take him on a mystery tour of the sights around your area. Take her to the races and watch her excitement as she backs her favourite horse. Don't forget that Sagittarians are mythical centaurs, so if you can't get to the race track, arrange for her to have a lesson at the nearest riding stables. And if you both ride, she'll adore a pony trek with you by her side, especially if you lay on a lavish picnic half-way through. And don't forget the champagne, she may be a tom-boy and a good sport but she does like to be spoilt and treated like a lady once in a while.

If your finances are tight, you could always buy your Archer sweetheart a glossy travel book – if they can't go physically on the journey, they're just as happy to go in their imagination. In fact, talking about imagination, Jupiter, the Sagittarian ruler, is the planet of expansion, so reading matter that will stretch their knowledge and understanding will be greatly appreciated (remember, books are a particular passion of Sagittarians).

Thinking of popping the question to your Sagittarian lady love? Then go for a ring with her special stones – turquoise and topaz are traditionally associated with this sign. And if you can save up enough to take her on a really fabulously romantic honeymoon, there would be nothing quite like a trip on the Orient Express to set this fiery lover alight.

HOLIDAYS

Sagittarians are born wanderers and a holiday for them means that they can indulge their passion for travel. They go where the muses take them, become excited with everything they encounter and in many ways, the journey for them is more exciting than the getting there. And if they get lost en route, what does it matter? There will be plenty to see anyway and masses to satisfy that well-known Sagittarian curiosity. In fact, the ambition of every Sagittarian has to be to go round the world at least once.

CAPRICORN

PRESENTS

Belonging to the element Earth, Capricorns have been described as conservative and traditional. They like presents that have a certain solidity and permanence about them. That's why antiques, even the smallest little treasure, will always please them. Pewter is the Capricornian metal so pewter trays, vases and snuff-boxes are appropriate.

They do have an eye for quality and, something that often comes as a surprise, Capricornians are drawn to status symbols – a hamper from Fortnum & Mason, gift vouchers from Selfridges, Liberty or Harrods, glossy coffee-table editions of art and fashion books, an annual subscription to 'Vogue' magazine.

If you're buying clothes for your Capricornian sweetheart, make sure they have a designer label in them. If they come from one of the Paris fashion houses, you'll really score a hit. The colours associated with this sign are sludge-browns and greens; greys and blacks, too, will suit. A touch of deep red would give a little relief to the darker shades and still be suitable.

People born at this point in the calendar, when one year gives way to another, have a special feel for time and they like watches, clocks, diaries and calendars. If you're buying the Capricorn man in your life anything in this line, keep the designer label in mind and buy the best quality you can afford. A Filofax is a brilliant idea and sure to please – but remember to write all your personal details, including your vital statistics, in it for him before you wrap it up.

Remember that this sign rules the skin, so you can't go wrong with cosmetics – as long, of course, as you choose the up-market brands. Capricorns are earthy, too, and many have green-fingers. Both men and women of the sign will be delighted with flowers, plants and seeds, either for indoors or for their gardens.

If you want to make a really romantic gesture towards your Capricornian girlfriend, present her with a single red rose, an orchid as a corsage. And when you ask her to marry you, go for a garnet engagement ring, as this is the stone that comes under the rulership of her sign.

HOLIDAYS

The bug-bear of all Capricornians considering a holiday is that they can't stand inefficiency and incompetence. So, if they come up against unreliable train timetables, sloppy hotels or mismanagement of any sort, they simply see red. From the moment they set foot outside their front door they expect the taxi to arrive on time, the plane to take off as scheduled, the hotel to be run like a tight ship, and its staff bustling about like well-drilled soldiers.

As they are such hard workers, they find it quite difficult to really let go and relax on holiday, and probably spend a good deal of the time looking around and picking-up all sorts of information that will be useful to them when they get back to their own work.

AQUARIUS

PRESENTS

When it comes to giving presents to an Aquarian it can be easy to make mistakes because they, of all the members of the Zodiac, have the most capricious likes and dislikes. Basically, Aquarians fall into two camps – either they are staunch traditionalists or they are ultra-modern. Size-up your Aquarian lover before deciding on a present to avoid getting the wrong thing.

Your traditionalist Aquarian lover will go a bundle on silks and satins, on wood and pure, new wool. They love glass and crystal, so a glass inscribed with their initials or a beautifully-cut decanter would please immensely.

They are great readers and love collecting books. A set of classics, especially if they are leather-bound, would delight your Aquarian sweetheart. You would be sure that she would think of you lovingly every time she turned the gilt-edged pages or proudly dusted them on her shelf. But they don't need to be expensive: a set of paperbacks, Jane Austin, Thackery, Agatha Christie, Conan-Doyle, all will be loved not only because books are special to them but, of course, because they came from you. For the more progressive Aquarian partner, think of science-fiction or modern writers, especially those with an individualistic slant to their style.

The more modern Aquarians can have the oddest tastes. If it's the latest craze, the most recent gadget, the newest invention to hit the market, buy it, wrap it and give it to your Aquarian heart-throb and watch the delight in their eyes. If it's kitsch, they'll flip their lids. Think of ultra-modern sunspecs, for instance, or rather *outré* jangly jewellery. Buy your Aquarian hunk a fouton, roll it out and roll yourselves in!

Clothes, as long as they are far-out, will be adored by the modernist, but don't make that mistake with your trad Water-bearer. For them it has to be classical and no messing. But, whether right in the front row with the latest trend-setters, or bringing-up the rear with the Establishment, they will go for electric blue. Buy her a vivid silk scarf, an azure T-shirt, blue suede shoes. For him, a classical tie with just a hint of electric blue, or jazz up his wardrobe with bright blue socks and shocking-blue braces.

Aquamarine and the lovely amethyst, so popular with Victorians, are specially associated with this sign. Old-fashioned or ultra-modern, an engagement ring with either of these stones will be sure to delight.

HOLIDAYS

Aquarians are extremely individualistic, with a certain unpredictability, which they like reflected in their holidays. They wouldn't for one moment go for the ordinary run-of-the-mill, package deal. Rather, because they are choosy people, they aim for something more unusual, locations that are tucked-away, maybe slightly difficult to get to, and less crowded.

Being unpredictable, they like to take-off on a whim, so need to feel free to pack a few things into a case and just go. And whilst on holiday, if they hear about a fascinating location on the other side of the island or at the other end of the country they might, on impulse, decide to visit it there-and-then.

PISCES

PRESENTS

Sensitive, sentimental Pisceans adore anything that smacks of nostalgia and romance.

Delightful antique trinkets are always a treat for them. If you're ever at an antique sale or fair think about your Piscean sweetheart. Pick-up a pretty lace collar or a beaded Victorian evening bag for her, a Wedgwood bowl for him, which you could fill with scented flower petals and place on his hall table.

Pisceans like to feel soft and cuddly, so if you want to buy them clothes look for sumptuous, soft fabrics, angora for her and cashmere for him. Muted colours suit them best; don't make the mistake of buying anything too garish, it's just too harsh against their delicate complexions. Instead, go for pale blues and greens, gentle silver-greys or barely-perceptible pinks.

As there is an association between this sign and feet, think about socks; these can range from traditional Scottish patterns, to thermal ones. Slippers for both your enchanting sweetheart or your hunky heart-throb will always be appreciated as their feet can be a constant source of discomfort. And what about a delicious electric footbath for them to sink their weary feet into after a long, hot day? Or book a foot massage, a session with a reflexologist or with a aromatherapist.

Delicate scents please them enormously. Lavender water, delightfully old-fashioned, would be just right for your Aquarian partner, especially if you pour it into a Victorian cut-glass atomiser. Think about toiletries for him, fresh and sharp and reminiscent of waves crashing on to a rocky shore, or tangy streams bubbling through a pine forest. A really romantic gift would be bath oil and a box of fragrant talc complete with soft, fluffy duster – and offer to apply it for her after her bath. . . .

Remember that Pisces is the sign of the Fishes, so if you're ever stuck, the fish motif, shells, mermaids or anything reminiscent of rivers and seas should stand you in good stead. Crystal, aquamarine, sapphire and emerald are all stones associated with this sign.

HOLIDAYS

Take a Piscean anywhere that's near water for a truly memorable holiday. It matters little whether it is on the Atlantic coast, by a babbling brook in the Quantock Hills or beside a glacial lake high in the Alps, as long as there is water in any shape or form, the Piscean will be happy.

Peace and tranquillity are also salient requirements for a Piscean holiday. That, and a fair bit of sun for good measure; lying on a Mediterranean island, with the clear blue water gently lapping at her feet, would make Ms Pisces feel she was in seventh heaven!

They need a touch of magic, too, to complete the child-like wonder of the Piscean temperament, a bit of nostalgia or exotic spice. So, add a touch of romance and the recipe is complete.